Contents

Rosso

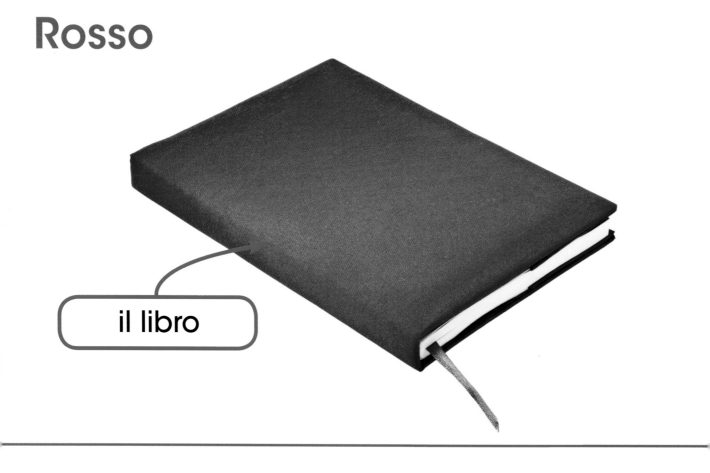

il libro

Il libro è rosso.

The book is red.

World Languages

Colours in Italian

Daniel Nunn

www.raintreepublishers.co.uk
Visit our website to find out more information about Raintree books.

To order:
☎ Phone 0845 6044371
🖷 Fax +44 (0) 1865 312263
🖳 Email myorders@raintreepublishers.co.uk

Customers from outside the UK please telephone +44 1865 312262

Raintree is an imprint of Capstone Global Library Limited, a company incorporated in England and Wales having its registered office at 7 Pilgrim Street, London, EC4V 6LB – Registered company number: 6695582

Edited by Daniel Nunn, Rebecca Rissman, and Sian Smith
Designed by Joanna Hinton-Malivoire
Picture research by Elizabeth Alexander
Production by Alison Parsons
Originated by Capstone Global Library Ltd
Printed in China

ISBN 978 1 406 23922 5 (hardback)
16 15 14 13 12
10 9 8 7 6 5 4 3 2 1

ISBN 978 1 406 23929 4 (paperback)
17 16 15 14 13
10 9 8 7 6 5 4 3 2 1

British Library Cataloguing in Publication Data
Nunn, Daniel.
  Colours in Italian. -- (World languages. Colours)
  1. Italian language--Vocabulary--Juvenile literature.
  2. Colors--Juvenile literature. 3. Italian language--
  Textbooks for foreign speakers--English.
  I. Title II. Series
  458.2'421-dc23

Acknowledgements
We would like to thank Shutterstock for permission to reproduce photographs: pp.4 (© Phiseksit), 5 (© Stephen Aaron Rees), 6 (© Tischenko Irina), 7 (© Tony Magdaraog), 8 (© szefei), 9 (© Picsfive), 10 (© Eric Isselée), 11 (© Yasonya), 12 (© Nadezhda Bolotina), 13 (© Maryna Gviazdovska), 14 (© Erik Lam), 15 (© Eric Isselée), 16 (© Ruth Black), 17 (© blueskies9), 18 (© Alexander Dashewsky), 19 (© Michele Perbellini), 20 (© Eric Isselée), 21 (© Roman Rvachov).

Cover photographs reproduced with permission of Shutterstock: dog (© Erik Lam), strawberry (© Stephen Aaron Rees), fish (© Tischenko Irina). Back cover photograph of a cake reproduced with permission of Shutterstock (© Ruth Black).

We would like to thank Nino Puma for his invaluable assistance in the preparation of this book.

Every effort has been made to contact copyright holders of material reproduced in this book. Any omissions will be rectified in subsequent printings if notice is given to the publisher.

la fragola

La fragola è rossa.

The strawberry is red.

Arancione

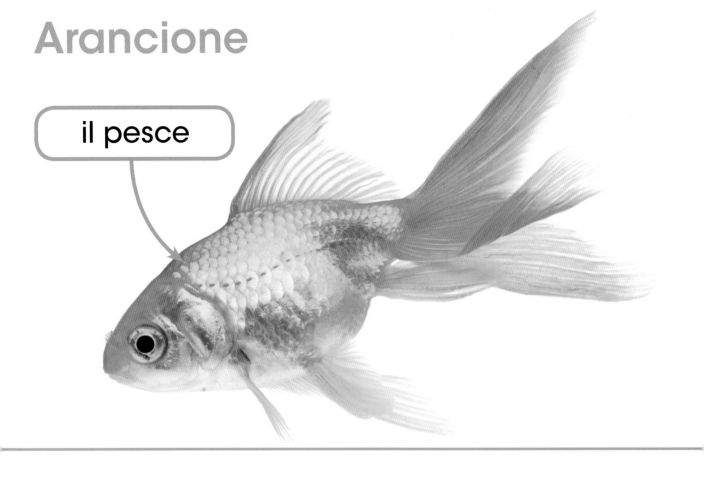

il pesce

Il pesce è arancione.

The fish is orange.

la carota

La carota è arancione.

The carrot is orange.

Giallo

il fiore

Il fiore è giallo.

The flower is yellow.

La banana è gialla.

The banana is yellow.

Verde

l'uccello

L'uccello è verde.

The bird is green.

la mela

La mela è verde.
The apple is green.

Blu

la maglietta

La maglietta è blu.

The T-shirt is blue.

la tazza

La tazza è blu.

The cup is blue.

Marrone

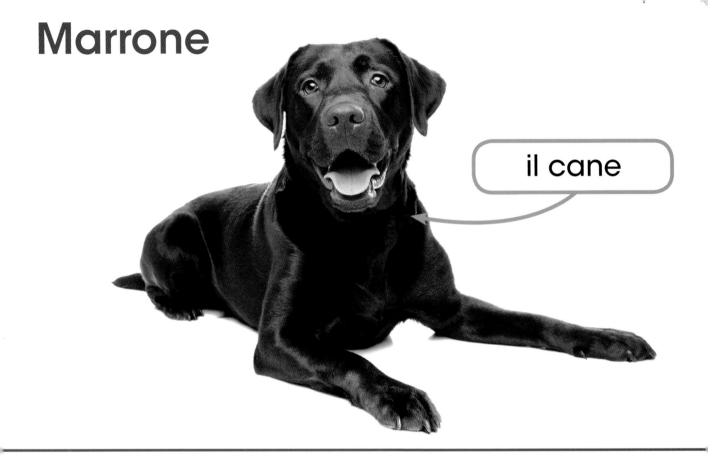

il cane

Il cane è marrone.

The dog is brown.

La mucca è marrone.

The cow is brown.

Rosa

il pasticcino

Il pasticcino è rosa.

The cake is pink.

il cappello

Il cappello è rosa.

The hat is pink.

Bianco

il latte

Il latte è bianco.

The milk is white.

la neve

La neve è bianca.

The snow is white.

Nero

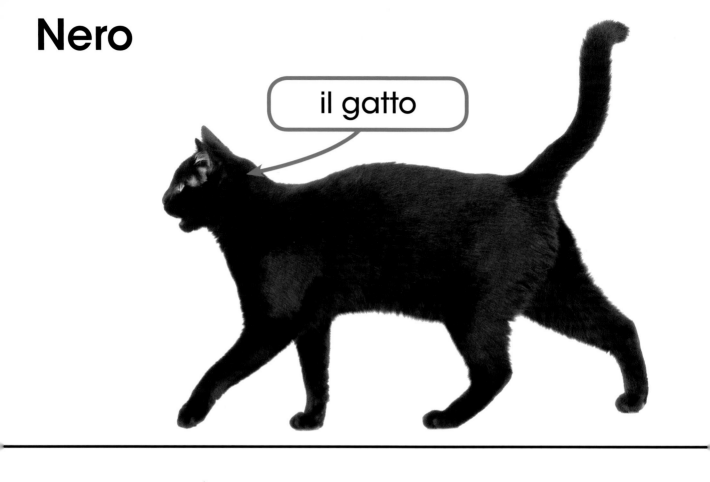

Il gatto è **nero**.

The cat is **black**.

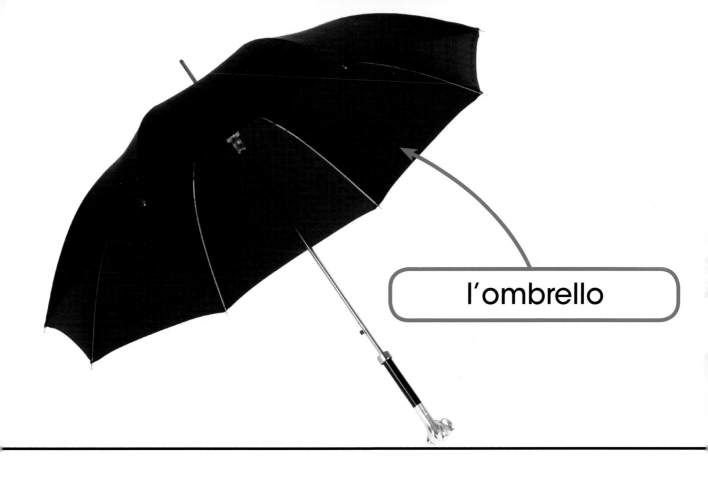

l'ombrello

L'ombrello è **nero**.

The umbrella is **black**.

Dictionary

Italian word	How to say it	English word
arancione	ar-ran-choh-nay	orange
banana	baa-naa-naa	banana
bianco/bianca	be-an-koh/be-an-kah	white
blu	bloo	blue
cane	ka-nay	dog
cappello	kap-pel-loh	hat
carota	kar-rot-ta	carrot
è	eh	is
fiore	fee-oar-ay	flower
fragola	fragg-o-lah	strawberry
gatto	gat-toh	cat
giallo/gialla	jal-loh/jal-la	yellow
il	eel	the (masculine)
la	lah	the (feminine)
latte	lat-tay	milk
libro	lee-broh	book

Italian word	How to say it	English word
maglietta	mah-lee-ay-tah	T-shirt
marrone	mar-roh-nay	brown
mela	meh-lah	apple
mucca	moo-kah	cow
nero	nare-oh	black
neve	nay-vay	snow
ombrello	ohm-brey-loh	umbrella
pasticcino	pa-stee-chee-noh	cake
pesce	peh-shay	fish
rosa	roh-sa	pink
rosso/rossa	ros-so/ros-sa	red
tazza	tah-tsa	cup
uccello	oo-chel-loh	bird
verde	vair-day	green

See words in the "How to say it" columns for a rough guide to pronunciations.

Index

Notes for parents and teachers

In Italian, nouns are either masculine or feminine. The word for "the" changes accordingly – either il (masculine) or la (feminine). Sometimes adjectives have different spellings too, depending on whether the noun is masculine or feminine. This is why some of the colours have more than one spelling.